The 5-Minute Meditation Journal

THE 5-MINUTE
MEDITATION
JOURNAL

QUICK GUIDED MEDITATIONS FOR
A CALMER, HAPPIER YOU

MIRANDA LEE

ROCKRIDGE
PRESS

Interior and Cover Designer: Diana Haas
Art Producer: Sara Feinstein
Editor: Eun H. Jeong
Production Editor: Sigi Nacson
Production Manager: Martin Worthington
Art used under license from Shutterstock.com. Author photo courtesy of Jennifer Almquist.

ISBN: 978-1-64876-983-2
R0

THIS JOURNAL BELONGS TO:

_____

CONTENTS

YOU CAN'T STOP THE WAVES,
BUT YOU CAN LEARN TO SURF.

—JON KABAT-ZINN, FROM *WHEREVER
YOU GO, THERE YOU ARE: MINDFULNESS
MEDITATION IN EVERYDAY LIFE*

Introduction

I am so glad that you have picked up this book and made the decision to begin, continue, or restart a meditation practice. I have found that people come to meditation for different reasons—to find help dealing with stress, anxiety, or depression, or for help to be more positive or productive in their daily life. I have also found that everyone can benefit from meditation, the practice of turning inward and learning about ourselves in a profound way.

When we know ourselves better, we can make better choices in our lives. When we pause to respond to the events of our lives rather than react automatically, we understand how much freedom to choose we have. It is this understanding of ourselves that helps us grow and change.

To achieve the benefits of meditation, we do not need to meditate for a long time each day. In this journal, I keep the meditations to five minutes long. What is more important than duration is working toward a consistent practice, so try to do one meditation and one journal entry each day. Then try to follow the intention for that meditation during your day. In this way, you can start to incorporate what you learn from each meditation into your life.

I teach these short but consistent practices because they have really helped me. I have been practicing meditation for more than 20 years, but it was when I was a busy mother of young kids, with very little time to myself, that I experienced the biggest transformation from meditation. Practicing short pauses throughout my day allowed me to connect better to myself, and this led to feeling much less overwhelmed. I hope you too can experience the rich rewards of a meditation practice, even with a busy schedule.

Finding a comfortable way to sit is important for meditation. I suggest finding a way to sit that enables you to breathe freely. Your eyes can be closed or open—see what works for you in quieting your mind. You might also like to sit in the same place every day, so it becomes your "meditation seat." This is your place to "be," and it's important that you do it in a way that feels right to you.

Meditation is a practice, so when you begin you may have moments of discomfort. Sometimes there are "aha" moments, and sometimes there is a slow unfolding of understanding. Be patient and kind with yourself on this amazing journey in self-discovery!

JOY AND CONNECTION

Sometimes we may feel that we are always chasing happiness and joy outside of ourselves. With the tools of meditation, we can start to be more aware of how much we already have in our lives. By connecting better to ourselves and understanding who we are and how we respond to the events of our lives, we can see the joy that is already here—the joy in the everyday things that we can so easily overlook in the busyness of life. As we connect better with ourselves, we can connect better with others. Through this new awareness, we can find more joy in the life we are already living, just by noticing more of what and who is around us.

I am a breathing body, I am a warm body

1. Find a comfortable way to sit.

2. Bring attention to your breath.

3. Take three deep breaths. Feel yourself breathing in your body.

4. Bring your attention to your heart. Can you feel your heart beating?

5. Bring your attention to your fingertips. Can you feel the blood pumping?

Have you ever noticed your body breathing before? Have you ever noticed your blood circulating in your body? How does it make you feel?

I will see what happens when I bring attention to my physical self during my day.

Connecting to yourself through the breath

1. Find a comfortable way to sit.

2. Bring attention to your breath.

3. Notice where in your body you feel the sensations of breathing. You may feel the breath in the flow of air at the nostrils or in the rise and fall of the belly or chest.

4. When you notice your mind wandering from the breath, which is normal, gently guide your attention back to the breath.

Were you aware of how your mind is constantly wandering? How did it feel when you brought your attention back to the breath?

As I move through my day, I will try to take moments to focus on my breath and see how that feels to me.

Connecting to the present moment

1. Find a comfortable way to sit.

2. Bring attention to your breath moving in and out of your body.

3. As you notice yourself taking an inhale, start counting 1, and for the next inhale count 2.

4. Continue counting your inhales to a count of 10, then start over again at 1.

5. When you notice your mind wandering and "thinking," start the count again.

6. Notice how long your mind is wandering before you remember to come back to the breath.

Were you surprised at how hard it is to count to 10 without your mind wandering? What did you find yourself thinking about?

I am thinking all the time, but I can choose to use the breath to be in the present moment.

Allowing yourself to "be"

1. Find a comfortable way to sit.

2. Bring attention to your breath and feel the physical sensations of breathing in the body.

3. Give yourself permission to just "be" here right now, knowing that there is no need to "do" anything.

4. If your mind starts to make plans or lists or starts "doing" things, see if you can gently redirect it back to feeling the breath.

5. Notice what emotions come up for you and label them, such as "this is frustrating," "this is calming," "this is releasing," and so on.

Write down how this meditation made you feel. Do you feel connected to yourself? Do you ever allow yourself just to "be" in your everyday life?

I will experiment with allowing myself to "be" during my day and see if anything changes for me.

Finding joy in the body

1. Find a comfortable way to sit.

2. Think about a time when you felt joy. It might be a time when you were enjoying a special activity, playing with a pet, or spending time with a good friend. Go with whatever comes to your mind.

3. Bring attention to your body at this moment of joy. Are you smiling? Do you feel a sense of warmth or spaciousness in your body?

4. Savor these feelings.

Where did you feel the sensations of joy in your body?
Did this surprise you?

_When I feel joy, I will notice the sensations of joy in my
body to appreciate it more fully._

Finding joy through your senses: sight

1. Find a comfortable way to sit.

2. Take three deep breaths.

3. Visualize something that you have seen recently that brought you joy: perhaps a beautiful object, a view of nature, or seeing a loved one smile.

4. Hold this image. With your mind's eye, notice the colors, textures, size, and shape.

5. Notice if any sensations in your body are changing and, if so, where you are feeling them.

Write down what you saw in the visualization. Use as many descriptive words as you can for what you saw.

_____

_____

_____

_____

_____

_____

_____

_____

_____

_____

_____

_____

_____

In my life, I can find joy through what I see. I will look for
the beautiful things in my life to bring me more joy.

Finding joy through your senses: sound

1. Find a comfortable way to sit.

2. Consider a sound in your life that makes you happy; perhaps it's a bird song, the sound of cooking, a piece of music, or the sound of children playing. Think of something that resonates for you.

3. Ask yourself why this sound makes you feel joyful. Is it the association of the sound to a pleasant memory, time, or person, or that the tone or melody is pleasant?

4. Sit and savor the feeling of this joyful sound.

Until you brought attention to this sound, would
you have noticed it brought you joy? What other
sounds bring you joy?

_____

_____

_____

_____

_____

_____

_____

_____

_____

_____

_____

_____

_____

In my life I can find joy through what I hear. I will notice
the sounds in my life that make me happy.

Finding joy through your senses: taste

1. Choose a snack that you enjoy, such as a piece of fruit, some raisins, or mini marshmallows. Make sure there are a few pieces of the snack before you begin the practice.

2. Take a moment to really look at your snack, and notice how it makes you feel to anticipate eating it.

3. Take a bite of the snack, but don't chew yet; just notice how the food feels in your mouth.

4. Chew slowly, noticing how the taste changes with each chew.

5. Swallow slowly. Consider how you feel.

6. Repeat the practice a few times, eating each piece of the snack slowly.

Consider how much you enjoyed the snack. Was your enjoyment more or less than when you normally eat it?

_____

_____

_____

_____

_____

_____

_____

_____

_____

_____

_____

_____

_____

_____

_____

*When I slow down to really taste my food, I can
enjoy it more.*

Finding joy in nature

1. Start this practice when you find yourself outside where you can see some green space, such as a backyard, a park, or a nature spot. Take a short walk.

2. Bring your attention to slowing down and consciously noticing the sights, sounds, and smells around you.

3. Say to yourself, "I am seeing this, I am hearing this, I am smelling this."

4. Notice as many things as you can, no matter how small, especially what you observe as you slow down.

5. Bring your attention to how you feel inside your body at this time.

Write down as many things as you can remember that you saw, heard, and smelled on your walk. Describe how these things made you feel.

_____

_____

_____

_____

_____

_____

_____

_____

_____

_____

_____

_____

_____

When I walk in nature I will try to slow down for a few
moments to savor the sights, sounds, and smells.

Connecting to others through mindful listening

1. Start this practice when you are speaking to someone you would like to better connect with.

2. While they are speaking, bring your full attention to what they are saying.

3. Try to stay in the present moment, listening rather than jumping ahead to how you will respond.

4. When they have finished speaking, take a breath, pausing to consider what they have said before you respond.

How was the conversation different when you practiced mindful listening? How did the other person respond?

_____

_____

_____

_____

_____

_____

_____

_____

_____

_____

_____

_____

I will listen mindfully when I want to connect
better with others.

Connecting to "YOU"

1. Find a comfortable way to sit.

2. Bring your attention down from your head into your body, and feel your whole body breathing.

3. Consider all the responsibilities in your life, such as being a worker, parent, child, and so on.

4. See if you can allow yourself to remove these feelings of responsibility just for a few minutes, like you are peeling them away from your body.

5. Consider the person who is left once these responsibilities are removed.

Describe the person you found when your responsibilities had been removed. How can you connect with that person more?

I will take a moment to connect with
who I am each day this week.

How the body tells me how I feel

1. Find a comfortable way to sit.

2. Take some deep breaths and feel them in the body.

3. Bring your attention to your body and investigate if your body gives you any information on how you are feeling right now. For example, is anywhere tight? Is anywhere feeling open and spacious?

4. Try to notice any subtle feelings and make sure you explore all over your body to see what it is telling you.

What sensations did you notice in your body? Where in the body did you feel them? Have you ever considered the body as a place to feel emotions before?

_____

_____

_____

_____

_____

_____

_____

_____

_____

_____

_____

_____

The body holds my emotions—I will listen to the body to know how I feel.

I am feeling . . .

1. Find a comfortable way to sit.

2. Bring attention to the body and consider what it is telling you about how you feel.

3. Label that feeling, beginning with, "I am feeling . . ."

4. Notice where in the body you are feeling it. Be as specific as you can, even bringing a hand to the place where you feel it.

5. Sense if the emotion feels warm or cool, light or heavy, rough or smooth in the body.

What emotion did you feel in the body? Describe how it felt. Does this tell you anything about the emotion?

_____

_____

_____

_____

_____

_____

_____

_____

_____

_____

_____

_____

*I recognize that I feel emotion in my body. As I
become more aware of sensations in my body, I will be
more aware of how I am feeling.*

Joy and sorrow are inseparable

1. Find a comfortable way to sit.

2. Consider a time in your life when you have felt joy.

3. Bring yourself into that moment of joy.

4. Now consider a time when you have felt sorrow.

5. Bring yourself into that moment of sorrow.

6. Take a moment to consider this: The poet Kahlil Gibran said that we only emotionally understand joy and sorrow because we have felt them both, which means that without one we could not feel the other.

Do you agree that our emotions are all connected? Does it make sense to you that when we try not to feel one we cannot feel another?

_____

_____

_____

_____

_____

_____

_____

_____

_____

_____

_____

_____

*I will allow myself to feel all my emotions, because without
one I cannot feel another.*

Connecting with others

1. Find a comfortable way to sit.

2. Take a few deep breaths.

3. Consider what it has felt like to connect with yourself using meditations in this chapter.

4. Use your knowledge of connecting with yourself to consider how you could connect with others in a more meaningful way.

Consider the people in your life. Are there any whom
you would like to connect with more? Describe what you
could do to have this connection.

I will be more aware of the power of connection in my life.

2

CALM AND FOCUS

Meditation practice teaches us that taking small pauses throughout our busy days can help reduce stress and calm us down. One reason is because pausing is good for our nervous system. We spend a lot of time "doing," but our nervous system also needs us to slow down and spend time just "being" in order to recalibrate and be in balance. As we learned in chapter 1, we always have the ability to refocus our mind back to the breath to find a moment of peace. But it's hard to integrate this into our lives without regular practice. The meditations in this chapter are short ways to practice finding that pause during your day.

Another benefit of meditation is the increased awareness that we have the power to choose where we place our attention. In this way we can learn to focus on what we want, rather than having our mind constantly wandering throughout our day. This chapter will give some examples of how to do this, helping us be more present in our lives.

Using a still and quiet body to calm yourself

1. Find a comfortable way to sit.

2. Focus on sitting as quietly and as still as you can.

3. Notice the sensations of breathing, your heart beating, and the blood pumping through your body.

4. Notice the stillness of your body; how does it make you feel?

5. Notice the quietness around you; how does it make you feel?

Describe how coming to a still and quiet sitting position made you feel. Did it change how you felt emotionally? If so, in what way?

_____

_____

_____

_____

_____

_____

_____

_____

_____

_____

_____

_____

_____

Throughout my day, I will try pausing and being in
my still body for a few minutes.

Calming breath

1. Find a comfortable way to sit.

2. Bring your attention to your breath, taking some deeper and longer breaths.

3. As you breathe in, count slowly to 3 or 4.

4. As you breathe out, count slowly to 5 or 6.

5. Don't force the breath; see what length of breath feels comfortable to you.

6. Notice the rhythm of the breath, where it starts, how it moves through the body, and when it ends. Notice the pause between the breaths.

7. After 10 of these longer breaths, notice how you feel.

What changes did you feel between the beginning and the end of the practice? Why do you think that was?

_____

_____

_____

_____

_____

_____

_____

_____

_____

_____

_____

_____

_____

When I feel unsettled, I will use my calming
breath to soothe myself.

Using your anchor

1. Find a comfortable way to sit.

2. Bring your hand to your belly and feel the contraction and expansion of your belly as you breathe.

3. Imagine that focusing on your breath in your belly is like an anchor for a ship at sea. When your mind starts to float you away, you can come back to the present moment using your anchor.

4. As you notice yourself thinking (and you will!), gently bring your attention back to the physical sensations of the breath in your body.

Think about how your mind feels when you are stressed. Does it feel like you are in a storm? How can this meditation practice help you anchor yourself and calm the storm?

_____

_____

_____

_____

_____

_____

_____

_____

_____

_____

_____

_____

_____

_____

*I will use my breath as an anchor when I need to
let go of stressful thinking.*

Your mind is like a butterfly

1. Find a comfortable way to sit.

2. Bring your attention to the sensations of breathing in your body.

3. Notice when your attention starts to flutter away from the breath. Then, like coaxing a butterfly back into a butterfly house, bring your attention back to your breath.

4. Continue doing this for five minutes, coaxing your mind back to the breath each time.

Write down some times in your life when you have noticed your mind is fluttering around like a butterfly. How do you think this practice can help you in your life?

_____

_____

_____

_____

_____

_____

_____

_____

_____

_____

_____

_____

I will be aware of how my mind is like a butterfly,
knowing that if I choose to, I can bring my mind back to
the present moment using the breath.

Mindfulness of sound

1. Pick a sound that you find is pleasant to listen to and is long lasting, such as a gong sound (see Resources on page 130 for sound apps).

2. Listen to the sound once through with your full attention.

3. Repeat this practice five times. Each time, notice if your mind wanders to "thinking" while you are listening to the sound.

4. Bring your attention back to the sound each time.

What did you learn from this practice? When you were able to focus on the sound, how did it make you feel?

_____

_____

_____

_____

_____

_____

_____

_____

_____

_____

_____

_____

_____

I will look for ways to bring my attention to sounds in my day-to-day life and see how it makes me feel.

Reducing stress in the body

1. Find a comfortable way to sit.

2. Take some long, deep breaths. Notice the physical sensation of breathing in your body.

3. Gently roll your shoulders away from your ears.

4. Gently massage your shoulders with your hands.

5. Bring your hands up to your face to massage any tension out of your jaw, eye sockets, and facial muscles.

6. Relax your tongue in your mouth and your eyes in their sockets.

7. Notice if anything shifted in how you feel.

Did you feel any tension release when you started this practice? If so, where in your body was it released from?

_____

_____

_____

_____

_____

_____

_____

_____

_____

_____

_____

_____

*I will notice when my body is tense and spend some time
each day working to release the tension.*

My thoughts pass by like clouds in the sky

1. If the day is nice, go outside and lie down, if possible, so you can watch the clouds. If the weather doesn't permit this, watch the clouds looking out a window.

2. Really pay attention to the clouds. What shapes are they? Do they look like something to you? How are they moving?

3. Describe them to yourself.

4. Stay for a few minutes, really paying attention to the clouds moving in the sky.

How are your thoughts like clouds? Do they pass through your mind? Do some stay? If you allow them to drift away like a cloud in the sky, do they?

_____

_____

_____

_____

_____

_____

_____

_____

_____

_____

_____

_____

_____

If I find myself thinking about the same thought again and again, I can let it go like a cloud passing in the sky.

Watching my emotions pass through me

1. Find a comfortable way to sit.

2. Ask yourself how you are feeling today and see what emotion comes up for you.

3. Label the emotion to yourself, "I feel . . ." and then say to yourself, "This too will pass."

4. Move on to another emotion and repeat step 3.

5. As you cycle through this process, see if any of the emotions have passed through your body and you no longer feel them.

Think about when you feel an emotion. Could you use this practice to allow it to pass through you? How could this be helpful?

_____

_____

_____

_____

_____

_____

_____

_____

_____

_____

_____

_____

When I feel emotions in my body, I know they
will pass through me.

Shaking my emotions through me

1. Stand with your feet planted firmly on the ground. (If standing is difficult, sit in a chair that allows your feet to rest firmly on the ground.)

2. Notice how you are feeling emotionally.

3. Now start gently shaking the lower body, starting with your feet, then lower legs, and thighs. Then move up to the upper body, starting with your hips, then stomach, shoulders, arms, and head. Finally, move your facial muscles and jaw, and roll your eyes in their sockets.

4. Continue shaking the whole body for a minute or so— the longer the better.

5. Stop and immediately notice any shifts or changes in how you feel emotionally.

Did this shaking shift how you felt? If yes, how so?
Sometimes emotions get stuck in the body and need to
be released through movement. Did this happen for you?
If you didn't experience a change in how you felt, that's
okay. Try this practice again another day and see if you
notice a difference.

I know that shaking my body can help me
release my emotions.

Is it true?

1. Find a comfortable way to sit.

2. Take some deep, very long breaths.

3. Notice the sensations of breathing in the body. Anchor yourself in the breath.

4. As thoughts come up, notice them and consider what they are saying. Ask yourself if those thoughts are true.

5. Gently bring your attention back to the breath.

6. Stay with this practice for five minutes.

What did you discover about your thoughts from the practice? Were your thoughts factual or fictional? What does that mean to you?

As thoughts come up in the day, especially stressful thoughts, I can consider if they are true or not true. If they are not true, I can let them go.

Mindful movement

1. Find a comfortable way to sit.

2. Bring both your hands to your lap and close your eyes.

3. Very slowly, and very gradually, lift one of your arms up in front of you.

4. Notice if your arm feels heavy or light.

5. Notice if you can feel the shape of your hand with your eyes closed.

6. Notice if there are any feelings of warmth, cold, or heat.

7. Gradually bring your arm back down. Notice any changes you feel.

8. Repeat the action with the other arm. Was there any difference from one arm to the other?

Were you surprised by anything you noticed in moving slowly and mindfully? Describe what this was. How did it make you feel to move like this?

When I move mindfully, I can shift how I feel.

Mindful walking

1. Stand up mindfully—that is, slowly and with attention on each movement.

2. As you breathe in, lift a foot and move it forward.

3. As you breathe out, place the foot down in front of you.

4. Take a few steps like this.

5. Continue walking mindfully, but now as you take a step forward, focus on the bottom of the foot as you walk. Notice how it feels on the ground, being lifted up, and being placed back down.

6. Continue walking mindfully for five minutes.

What did it feel like to walk mindfully? How could it be useful to you? How does it differ from how you normally walk?

_____

_____

_____

_____

_____

_____

_____

_____

_____

_____

_____

_____

_____

*I will try to take a few mindful steps each day
and notice how it feels.*

Mindful seeing

1. Find a comfortable way to sit.

2. Take a few deep breaths to settle yourself.

3. Look around the room and find an everyday object to focus on, such as a piece of furniture, the carpet, or something small.

4. Really focus on this object; consider its colors, textures, and shapes.

5. Focus on it for a few minutes, even if your mind is asking you to move away.

6. Consider if you saw anything new in this object.

Describe what you saw in the object. Did you notice anything new about it? Consider how many times you have missed seeing this aspect of the object. What does this tell you?

_____

_____

_____

_____

_____

_____

_____

_____

_____

_____

_____

_____

_____

_____

I can choose to look more closely at my surroundings.
When I do, I may see something new and interesting.

Using your senses

1. Find a comfortable way to sit.

2. Take a few deep breaths to settle yourself.

3. Find five things you can see right now and label them to yourself; for example, "I see a table, I see a chair," and so on.

4. Identify five sounds you can hear right now and label them to yourself; for example, "I hear a car, I hear the air conditioner," and so on.

5. Consider five things you can feel right now; for example, the chair you are sitting on, the ground under your feet, or the clothing you are wearing.

Write down your lists of the five things you saw, heard, and felt. Were you surprised by any of them? How did it make you feel to do this practice?

When I focus on what is around me right now,
I can change how I am feeling.

Watching a candle flame

1. Take a seat in a dark room, with a lighted candle about two or three feet away from you.

2. Settle into your body and take a few deep breaths.

3. Focus your eyes on the flame of the candle.

4. Notice the colors and shape of the flame. Notice what happens when the flame flickers or moves.

5. Keep focusing on the flame for as long as your time allows.

6. Before you end the meditation, notice if there have been any shifts or changes in how you feel.

What did you notice when you stared at the candle? Did you notice anything else? Did you feel calmer? If so, why do you think that was?

I have the ability to focus on one thing. When I do that, it helps me feel calm and intentional.

3

AWAKE AND REST

Meditation can be done at any time during the day, but many people find that starting the day with a practice can be helpful. When we first wake up the mind is more settled, and we have fewer thoughts bouncing around inside. We can, therefore, be clearer in our thinking and less distracted. A morning meditation can also be a great time to set an intention for the day.

Meditation at the end of the day can also be helpful. It is when the mind is often at its busiest, making it difficult for us to unwind from the day. A few minutes of meditation at this time can help soothe our minds to enable us to more easily relax and get to sleep.

Setting an intention

1. As you wake up, gently place a hand on your heart and ask yourself what you most want in your life right now. Some phrases you could use are "May I find more joy today," "May I focus better today," or "May I pause more today." See if you can find a phrase that resonates for you.

2. Feel the intention pass from your mind to your heart.

3. Pause for a moment to acknowledge the intention before beginning your day.

Write down what your intention is for the day. At the end of the day, consider if the intention affected your day at all, and if so, how.

_____

_____

_____

_____

_____

_____

_____

_____

_____

_____

_____

_____

I can choose an intention for myself and how
I want to live each day.

Waking the body up mindfully

1. As you wake up in the morning, see if you can slowly bring your attention down to your feet.

2. Slowly scan the body from the feet up, gently "waking up" each part of the body with your mind. From the feet, go to the legs, then the hips, back, stomach, arms, shoulders, head, and finally the eyes.

3. Notice how it feels to greet your body this way.

Describe how it felt to wake your body up this way and how it felt different from how you usually wake up.

_____

_____

_____

_____

_____

_____

_____

_____

_____

_____

_____

_____

_____

_____

_____

I can choose how I wake myself up. When I do it with awareness, it sets me up for a mindful day.

Mindful breathing as you wake

1. As soon as you wake up, gently bring yourself to a comfortable sitting position.

2. Take three long, drawn-out breaths.

3. Start to anchor yourself in the physical sensations of breathing in your body.

4. As you start to notice yourself "thinking," bring yourself back to the breath. Continue for five minutes.

5. Notice if there is any difference in this practice when done at the beginning of the day or at a later time of the day.

Was your mind any different first thing in the morning? If so, what was different? Try this meditation at the end of the day and see if you notice any changes.

I will notice the way my mind changes through the day.

Greeting the sun

1. As soon as you wake up, find a place where you can see the sun.

2. Feel the warmth of the sun on your face.

3. Notice as many places as you can see being touched by the sun; for example, the sparkle of the sun on water, on building windows, and so on.

4. How does it make you feel to look at the sun shining?

5. Close your eyes and savor the feeling.

Did it feel different to you to start the day by greeting the sun? Describe how it felt.

_____

_____

_____

_____

_____

_____

_____

_____

_____

_____

_____

_____

_____

_____

By changing how I start my day, I can change how
I feel about my day.

Saluting the sun

1. As soon as you wake up, find a place where you can see the sun.

2. Stand looking in the direction of the sun. (If standing is difficult, sit in a chair that allows your feet to rest firmly on the ground.)

3. Breathe in and raise your hand(s) above your head.

4. As you breathe out, bend your knees, fold forward, and allow your arms to hang down toward the floor. (If this is difficult, skip this step and the next, and repeat step 3 three times but lower your arms as you breathe out.)

5. On the next inhaled breath, roll up with a rounded spine to bring yourself to a standing position.

6. Repeat the exercise three times.

How did it feel to greet the sun and welcome the day in this way? How did it feel to be aware of breathing and moving at the same time?

_____

_____

_____

_____

_____

_____

_____

_____

_____

_____

_____

_____

When I acknowledge the sun first thing in the morning, my day feels different.

Greeting the day with gratitude

1. As soon as you wake up, take a deep breath.

2. Think of three things you are grateful for in this moment. They may be small things, such as enjoying a good night's sleep, or a bigger thing, like having a warm home to sleep in.

3. Appreciate these things you are grateful for before getting up.

Write down the three things you are grateful for today.
How did it make you feel to wake up in this way?

_____

_____

_____

_____

_____

_____

_____

_____

_____

_____

_____

_____

_____

I can choose to wake up feeling grateful.

Starting the day without distractions

1. As you wake up, make a conscious effort to not look at your screen devices (phones, computers, etc.).

2. Take a few deep breaths. If you like, choose one of the waking meditations from earlier in this chapter, but ensure you take at least a few minutes to yourself.

3. After a few minutes, start your day.

Write down how you feel before you look at a device. After you have checked your device and looked at your messages, notifications, and so on, write down how you feel. Was there a change?

_____

_____

_____

_____

_____

_____

_____

_____

_____

_____

_____

_____

_____

_____

I can take some time for myself first thing in the morning to change how I feel about my day.

Bringing it all together

1. As you wake up, make a conscious effort to not look at your screen devices (phones, computers, etc.).

2. Take a few breaths and set a simple intention for yourself.

3. Look out a window. Take a moment to feel the warmth of the sun and enjoy something that you see.

4. Move your body in any way that feels good to you, such as a stretch, a shake, or a jump.

5. Take a moment to notice how you feel before you start your day.

Describe your morning routine, the intention you set, what you saw outside, and what movement you did. What effect did they have on how you were feeling?

_____

_____

_____

_____

_____

_____

_____

_____

_____

_____

_____

_____

_____

_____

_____

_____

*I have the freedom to start my day in a way that feels good
to me. It sets me up for the way I want to live my life.*

Sitting with your tiredness

1. When you are ready to go to sleep, find a comfortable seat for meditation.

2. Take three deep breaths.

3. Notice the places in your body that feel tired. Do your shoulders feel heavy? How about your arms and legs? Perhaps your eyes feel like they need to release.

4. Stay with these physical sensations of tiredness in your body for a few minutes.

5. Scan your body, looking again for any areas that are tired, breathing into those areas to release those physical sensations.

Where did you feel the physical sensations of tiredness in your body? How did it feel to release these sensations?

_____

_____

_____

_____

_____

_____

_____

_____

_____

_____

_____

_____

_____

_____

I can use my body to notice my tiredness and release it.

Mindful lying down

1. Lie down on the floor or on your bed.

2. Allow your feet to turn out and the palms of your hands to face up. Allow your arms and legs to relax.

3. Feel each part of the body touching the ground (or bed), from the feet to the legs, back, arms, and head. Release each into the ground (or bed), one by one.

4. Notice how it feels to relax into the gentle pull of gravity.

5. Take a moment to savor this feeling of just "being."

How did it feel to release your body into the ground (or your bed)?

_____

_____

_____

_____

_____

_____

_____

_____

_____

_____

_____

_____

When I feel tired, I can release my body.

Noticing "waking" thoughts and "resting" thoughts

1. Come into a mindful lying-down posture.

2. Bring your attention to the feeling of the breath coming in and out of your body.

3. Count each in-breath and each out-breath for a count of 10.

4. When you notice yourself thinking, see if you can ask yourself gently if it is a thought that will make you wake up or if it is one that will allow you to sleep.

5. When you have decided, follow the thought or bring your attention back to the breath, starting the count again at 1.

How difficult or easy was it to choose which thoughts would help you rest? Did the thoughts wake you up or make you sleepy?

_____

_____

_____

_____

_____

_____

_____

_____

_____

_____

_____

_____

I can choose to allow my mind to rest by choosing my thoughts.

Balloon breath

1. Come into a mindful lying-down posture.

2. Place an object, such as a small pillow or book, on your belly.

3. Breathe naturally, noticing the sensation of the object moving with each inhale and exhale.

4. Stay breathing like this for a few minutes.

5. Notice if you feel different at the end of the practice.

Describe how balloon breathing felt to you. Did it feel like a balloon expanding and contracting or like something else? Did it change how you felt emotionally?

_____

_____

_____

_____

_____

_____

_____

_____

_____

_____

_____

I can use balloon breathing to help settle my mind.

Tighten and release

1. Come into a mindful lying-down posture, releasing your body into the ground or your bed.

2. Take a deep breath in.

3. Starting with your feet and progressively moving up your body to your head, tighten each part of the body: feet, legs, hips, back, chest, arms, shoulders, jaw, facial muscles, and eyes. Hold for a second or two.

4. Release the body as you breathe out.

5. Repeat this exercise three times.

Notice how it felt at the end of the practice. Was there a place in your body that felt a sense of "release"? If so, where? Did you feel a sense of release in more than one area?

I can release my body before I rest to help me sleep.

Visualizing a calm place

1. Come into a mindful lying-down posture.

2. Scan your body. Release any tension you find.

3. Take some deep breaths.

4. Visualize a place or scene that feels calm to you. Some ideas may be a tropical beach, a forest, a mountain view, or a field of wildflowers swaying in a breeze.

5. Visualize yourself in this place. Really notice the scene in front of you—smell the smells and hear the sounds.

6. Savor this image.

Describe the place you chose. Why did you choose this place? What feelings did it bring up for you?

_____

_____

_____

_____

_____

_____

_____

_____

_____

_____

_____

_____

_____

_____

*I can decide to visualize a calming scene to
help me get ready to rest.*

I give myself permission to rest

1. Come into a mindful lying-down posture.

2. Choose the resting practice that you most enjoyed in this chapter: waking/resting thoughts, balloon breath, tighten and release, or visualizing a calm place. Start the practice.

3. As you go through the practice, set the intention "I give myself permission to rest."

4. Repeat this intention silently to yourself over and over again during the practice.

5. Notice any change in how you feel.

Did the practice change for you when you gave yourself permission to rest? Do you ever give yourself permission to rest?

_____

_____

_____

_____

_____

_____

_____

_____

_____

_____

_____

_____

_____

*I can give myself permission to rest in my life, so I can be
more productive when I am not resting.*

COMPASSION AND GRATITUDE

One of the greatest benefits of meditation practice is becoming more compassionate toward ourselves, especially when we go through challenging times. Feeling self-compassion can be uncomfortable at first if we are not used to it. However, many studies show that self-compassion can benefit us greatly, as well as allow us to be more compassionate toward others.

Meditation practices also allow us to focus better on the life that we are living right now. This focus enables us to see what we have to be grateful for in our lives, without needing to change anything apart from our mindset. We can start to see the smaller things to be grateful for that we may not normally notice, as well as the larger things. We become aware that sometimes it's the easily overlooked things in life that are, in the end, most meaningful to us.

I give myself permission to care for myself

1. Place a hand on your heart and close your eyes if that feels good.

2. As you feel the warmth of your hand on your heart, internally repeat an intention of giving kind attention to yourself. For example, you could say, "May I give myself kindness," "I give myself permission to care for myself," or "May I give myself love at this moment." Choose one of these intentions or create one of your own.

3. Sit with this practice, repeating the intention for a few minutes.

Write down the intention you chose. Why was it meaningful to you? Did anything change in how you felt doing this practice?

_____

_____

_____

_____

_____

_____

_____

_____

_____

_____

_____

_____

*I can give myself permission to care for myself,
and it helps me feel good.*

Loving-kindness practice

1. Think of someone kind in your life. They can be real, a fictional character, or a spiritual being.

2. Send them kind thoughts or repeat an intention of kindness to them. How does this feel to you?

3. Now see if you can visualize this person or being sending this kindness back to you. How does this feel?

4. Send this feeling of kindness from you out into the world. How does this feel to you?

Who did you choose to send kindness to? Was it easier for you to send kind thoughts to them or to visualize them sending kind thoughts to you? Why do you think this is?

_I can create more kindness in my life by using my mind
to send kind thoughts to others._

The compassionate friend

1. Visualize someone with a warm and compassionate presence, someone who is wise, strong, and loving. It may be someone you know or a spiritual or imaginary being. This is your compassionate friend.

2. Visualize you and your compassionate friend meeting.

3. As you visualize the two of you, feel that your friend cares deeply for you and would like for you to be happy and free from struggle.

4. Imagine that your friend tells you something you need to hear right now.

5. Savor being with your friend and hearing what they tell you.

What did your compassionate friend say to you? Why do you think you needed to hear that? Do you think your compassionate friend is actually a part of you?

I can visualize a compassionate friend to help me get through challenging times.

Self-compassion holding exercises

1. Bring your hands to your heart and gently massage your heart area. Take a few deep breaths.

2. Bring your hands to your shoulders and gently massage your shoulders, soothing any tension found there. Take a few deep breaths.

3. Place one hand behind your head below your skull. Move your other hand up to your forehead. Feel your head being supported by your hands. Take a few deep breaths.

When might a self-compassion practice like this be most helpful? Which self-compassion holding exercise did you prefer?

I can use my own soothing touch to bring
some compassion to myself.

Noticing our minds

1. Find a comfortable way to sit.

2. Bring your hands to your belly. Feel the contraction and expansion of your belly as you breathe.

3. When you notice yourself thinking, consider if it is a thought that is kind to you or not kind to you.

4. Bring your attention gently back to the breath.

5. Repeat this cycle of noticing the tendency of your mind and guiding yourself back to the breath again for a few more minutes.

What did you notice about the tendency of your mind?
Were your thoughts negative or positive toward you?
Why do you think this is?

_____

_____

_____

_____

_____

_____

_____

_____

_____

_____

_____

_____

_____

When I notice the negative tendency of my mind, I can
bring some kindness to myself.

The people who have helped me

1. Find a comfortable way to sit.

2. Take some deep breaths.

3. Visualize someone in your life who has helped you. It might be someone who was a big influence in your life, like a mentor or teacher, or someone who did a small kindness to you recently.

4. Send this person a kind intention or visualize telling them what they mean to you.

5. See if you can feel this sense of gratitude in the body and notice how it feels.

Write down the person you visualized and how they helped you. Then, write down what you said to express your gratitude and describe how it felt to express it.

When I notice the people in my life who have helped me, it makes me feel good.

Small generous acts

1. Find a comfortable way to sit.

2. Take some deep breaths.

3. Imagine yourself doing a small generous act for someone—not because you feel an obligation to do it, but simply because you want to. An example would be opening a door for someone carrying heavy bags, picking up something that someone has dropped, or saying something kind to someone.

4. Visualize yourself and the other person in this situation. Notice how you feel.

Write down what the act was and who it was for. Using as many descriptive words as you can, recount how doing this generous act made you feel.

_____

_____

_____

_____

_____

_____

_____

_____

_____

_____

_____

_____

When we are generous and kind to other people,
it makes us feel good.

Being grateful to someone you don't know

1. Gather some paper and a pen.

2. Start thinking about all the people you don't know in your life who have already helped you in your day so far: for example, the people who produced and transported your food to you, built the furniture around you, or produced the medicines you take. List as many of these people as you can.

3. Take a moment to review the list and think about how this list of people makes you feel.

How many people did you list? Did anyone on the list surprise you? Having written the list, do you feel more gratitude toward these people now? Why or why not?

_____

_____

_____

_____

_____

_____

_____

_____

_____

_____

_____

_____

_____

_____

_____

_____

I can feel gratitude even toward people I have not met.

Gratitude for our body

1. Find a comfortable way to sit.

2. Notice the quality of your breath. Is it easy for you to breathe at this time? Has there been a time when it was hard for you to breathe—for example, when you had a cough or a cold?

3. Savor the feeling of breathing well by taking a few deep breaths. Have you ever thought to be grateful for breathing easily?

4. Savor the feeling of being able to breathe well at this moment.

Are there other parts of your body you are grateful for right now? Note them here. For each one, explain why you are grateful.

_____

_____

_____

_____

_____

_____

_____

_____

_____

_____

_____

_____

_____

_____

*I can feel gratitude for my body and
notice what it is doing for me each day.*

Savoring the pleasant

1. Find a comfortable way to sit.

2. Visualize a time when you felt happy. Notice where you were, who you were with, and what you were doing. Try to recall the smallest details of the scene, such as the smells, the sounds, and even the color of the light.

3. Consider what you might have been thinking about during this time.

4. Try to feel the sensations of happiness in your body.

5. Sit and savor the feelings of this happy moment.

Describe the happy scene in as much detail as possible. Note any thoughts you had and physical sensations you felt during the visualization.

I will try to savor the happy times in my life, so when they pass, I can remember them clearly.

Finding gratitude in the everyday

1. Gather some paper and a pen.

2. Start thinking of small or large things in your life that you are grateful for today. Some examples would be your home, your bed to sleep in, electricity, the sun, a beautiful plant, your pet, and so on. These things may be personal to you or more general in nature.

3. Don't think too much about them—just write them down in a stream-of-consciousness way.

4. Write until you can't think of any more.

5. Take a moment to review your gratitude list.

How many things did you write down? Were you surprised by any of the things you wrote down? If so, why?

_____

_____

_____

_____

_____

_____

_____

_____

_____

_____

_____

_____

I can be grateful for many things each day.

Sharing gratefulness

1. Find a friend or family member who would be willing to do a gratefulness challenge with you.

2. Share with them three things you are grateful for at this moment, via text, e-mail, or a phone call. These things can be large or small.

3. Ask them to share with you three things they are grateful for.

4. If you like, continue the challenge for as many days as you both agree to.

How did you feel when you wrote down your three things? How did you feel when you read your friend's or family member's three things? Were your feelings similar or different?

_____

_____

_____

_____

_____

_____

_____

_____

_____

_____

_____

_____

_____

_____

Sharing my gratitude list with someone
makes me feel good.

Bringing self-compassion to a difficult moment

1. Bring to mind a situation that you are finding difficult in your life right now. (Do not bring to mind something really overwhelming.)

2. Get in touch with the situation by bringing your hand to your heart and saying the following phrases to yourself: "I am finding this situation challenging. Challenging moments are part of life. May I be kind to myself at this time." You may change the wording to make it more personal to you.

3. Repeat the phrases at least three times.

Did you notice any change in how you felt when you repeated these phrases? If so, what was the change? If you didn't notice a change in how you felt, return to this practice another day. Self-compassion can take time to develop.

_When I bring self-compassion to myself at a
difficult moment, I feel better._

Starting the day with kindness

1. As you wake up in the morning, place a hand on your heart and say the following intention to yourself: "May I be kind to myself today." You may change the wording to make it more personal to you.

2. Feel yourself bringing this intention inside yourself.

3. Repeat the practice each morning for as long as you feel comfortable, but ideally for a week.

At the end of the day, write down if you noticed any changes in your behavior that day. Were you kinder to yourself or others? If yes, in what ways? If you didn't notice any changes in your behavior, that's okay. Continue doing the meditation with the knowledge that behavior changes can take time.

When I make an intention to be kind to myself early in the morning, I am kinder all day.

Ending the day with gratitude

1. Before you go to sleep at night, write down three things you are grateful for at that moment. These things could be small or large.

2. Repeat this practice each night for as long as it feels comfortable to you, ideally for a week.

3. Each night, read the list from the previous night and see if it still holds true.

Did you notice any changes in how you felt from night to night when you wrote your gratitude list? Did the list stay the same or change as the week progressed?

When I write down those things for which I am grateful,
I see more things to be grateful for in my life.

MEDITATION PRACTICE ISN'T
ABOUT TRYING TO THROW
OURSELVES AWAY AND BECOME
SOMETHING BETTER. IT'S ABOUT
BEFRIENDING WHO WE ARE
ALREADY.

—PEMA CHÖDRÖN, FROM
THE WISDOM OF NO ESCAPE: HOW TO LOVE
YOURSELF AND YOUR WORLD

Closing Thoughts

My aim with this journal was to help you integrate small moments of meditation into your life. You do not need much time to pause and reflect to benefit from meditation. Have you noticed any changes in how you see yourself or your world yet?

In my experience, meditation has a subtle but profound way of changing our lives. It might be that the changes creep up on you. It may also take some time. This is because we are starting the change from the inside of us, out. At first, we may not notice much, but small incremental changes can add up to a profound difference in our lives over time.

Meditation is a very personal practice. Some of the practices in the journal you may have enjoyed; some may have been uncomfortable. I always tell my students, however, that each time you practice, you have had the practice you are meant to have at that time. It may be that being uncomfortable taught you something. It might also be worth trying each of the practices again to see if you feel the same way next time.

I hope that now that you have finished the journal, you want to continue practicing meditation. There are many ways to do this, and I have identified some apps and websites that I have found useful in the Resources (page 130). The most important thing for your meditation journey is to continue it. Meditation is a practice of keeping going, one step at a time. I wish you well on your journey!

Resources

Apps can be a helpful place to start with a meditation practice. Some offer timers, some free practices, some paid practices, some all three. These are the ones that I recommend:

Headspace is one of the first and best meditation apps.

Insight Timer has a great timer for personal practice, as well as a vast array of free classes and courses. These offerings make this app a great one to try first.

Ten Percent Happier has great teachers and courses led by journalist Dan Harris.

I recommend the following websites for content and resources, including courses and meditation books:

Greater Good has interesting information about meditation and other practices for leading happier, more resilient lives. They have a helpful newsletter and free happiness calendar you can sign up for. GreaterGood.berkeley.edu

Sounds True has some great online courses, as well as interesting meditation books for purchase. SoundsTrue.com/collections /meditation-music

Acknowledgments

Love and gratitude to my husband, Hyuk, who supported me in every way in writing this journal.

About the Author

 **Miranda Lee** teaches mothers, families, and kids how to lead contented and balanced lives using mindfulness and meditation techniques. With more than 20 years' experience as a yoga and meditation teacher, she considers her children to be her most important "Zen masters." They remind her daily of the importance of finding "that pause" in her life. More information on her teaching can be found on her website, FindThatPause.com. Follow her on Instagram: @find_that_pause.

CPSIA information can be obtained
at www.ICGtesting.com
Printed in the USA
JSHW020358080621
15657JS00011B/149